Stoic Public Speaking

Commanding Presence through Inner Calm

Table of Contents

Chapter 1. Introduction

Welcome to our Special Report: "Stoic Public Speaking: Commanding Presence through Inner Calm". This is not just another guide on public speaking; it is an invitation to embrace the stoic principles that can fundamentally transform how you communicate. Imagine holding the room, not by force but with an undeniable aura of calm and composure. Picture yourself making an indelible impact, delivering your thoughts with clarity, conviction, and authenticity, without any trace of fear or anxiety. Unearth the secrets to developing a strong, calm, and commanding presence that will keep your audience hanging on every word, all while maintaining inner peace. Because, effective public speaking isn't just about what you say, it's about who you are when you say it. Uplifting, practical and undeniably transformative, this report is essential reading for anyone who wishes to elevate their public speaking skills to unprecedented heights. Say goodbye to pre-speech jitters and hello to stoic serenity today!

Chapter 2. Discovering Your Inner Stoic: An Introduction

In our quest to achieve excellence in public speaking, we often overlook an integral component: our inner state. Indeed, mastering the tempo of your voice, curating the perfect words, and perfecting body language are necessary. Yet, achieving inner tranquility is a game-changer that affects all other aspects of public speaking.

2.1. Embracing the Philosophy

Stoicism, an ancient Greek philosophy, underpins this revolutionary approach to public speaking. Grounded in the teachings of Epictetus, Seneca, and Marcus Aurelius, among others, stoicism is about serenity in the face of adversity, maintaining inner calm irrespective of external circumstances, and focusing on what is within our control while letting go of what isn't.

This philosophy, adopted by some of history's greatest leaders and thinkers, is about being grounded in the present moment, irrespective of circumstances or situations that might trigger panic or fear - sentiments often associated with public speaking. By practicing stoicism, you can steady your mind, control your anxiety, and deliver your message with a calm, commanding presence that has the power to captivate, inspire, and influence.

2.2. Stoic Principles and Public Speaking

To understand how to integrate Stoicism into your public speaking, let's explore the core principles of this philosophy and how they apply to the art of speech-giving.

1. 1. The Dichotomy of Control: In Stoicism, it's understood that some things are in our control (our thoughts, beliefs, actions), and others are not (external events, other people's thoughts or actions, and the like). When it comes to public speaking, understanding this dichotomy allows us to focus our energies on what we can control. We cannot determine how the audience will react, but we can control our preparation, our delivery, and how we handle feedback.

2. 2. Living According to Nature: A fundamental principle of Stoicism is to live 'according to nature', which translated into the realm of public speaking, means speaking your truth, or being authentic in your communication. Authenticity is one of the most powerful tools in public speaking as the audience resonates more with speakers who are genuine, vulnerable, and real.

3. 3. Negative Visualization: Stoics advise practicing negative visualization, imagining the worst-case scenario, to maintain tranquility amidst adversity. For public speakers, this could mean visualizing stuttering or forgetting your speech, then preparing methods to recover smoothly.

4. 4. Virtue is the Highest Good: Stoicism holds that virtue (integrity, wisdom, courage, and justice) should be the ultimate goal. As a speaker, applying this principle means prioritizing your message's value and its benefit to the audience above all.

2.3. Exercises to Discover Your Inner Stoic

The practical application of stoicism is achieved through exercises designed to shift your mindset and build resilience. Here are a few exercises that can jump-start your journey towards stoic public speaking:

1. 1. Practice Mindfulness: Mindfulness strengthens your ability to

stay present and focused, cutting out distractions and anxiety. Start with five minutes of mindfulness a day - focus on your breath, body sensations, or sounds around you.

2. 2. Journaling: Stoic journaling exercise, known as "premeditatio malorum," involves writing down the worst things that can happen during your speech. This exercise helps resist the fear and prepares you for any outcome.

3. 3. Stoic Meditation: This variation of meditation involves contemplating Stoic principles, reflecting on how they apply to specific public speaking situations, and visualizing your application of these principles during speeches.

4. 4. Practise Rejection Therapy: It involves deliberately seeking out rejection to become comfortable with the feeling. The more you confront rejection, the less fear you'll feel about the possibility.

Embarking on this journey to discover and master your inner stoic isn't merely about enriching your public speaking skills; it's a step towards achieving a more balanced, courageous, and tranquil existence. As Marcus Aurelius, the trailblazer of stoicism, so elegantly stated, "You have power over your mind – not outside events. Realize this, and you will find strength."

Understanding and implementing stoic principles to public speaking takes one from merely delivering a speech to embodying a speaker—an infallible, calm, and authentic presence that can captivate and influence regardless of the situation or audience. To echo another stoic principle, we realize that our value as speakers isn't defined by applause or approval but by the authenticity of our message, the strength of our delivery, and the virtue of our intentions.

Chapter 3. The Stoic Philosophy and Its Connection to Effective Communication

The stoic philosophy was developed by several ancient Greek thinkers, but most prominently by Zeno of Citium in the 3rd century BC. Stoicism is a practical philosophy that focuses on developing one's virtue—especially wisdom, courage, justice, and temperance—to live a life free from suffering. It emphasizes the importance of understanding and accepting the nature of reality. Stoics believe that by recognizing the difference between what we can control and what we cannot, we can achieve inner peace. This understanding is highly beneficial in various aspects of life, including communication and public speaking.

3.1. Understanding Stoicism

Zeno's stoicism emphasizes four cardinal virtues of wisdom, courage, justice, and temperance. Wisdom helps us to make good decisions, courage enables us to face difficulties, justice prompts us to treat others fairly, and temperance keeps us from excesses. By cultivating these virtues, a Stoic aims to achieve 'eudaimonia' or a state of flourishing life.

Stoicism teaches us that our happiness lies in our response to external events, not the events themselves. According to Epictetus, "We cannot control what happens to us, but we can control how we react." Through this understanding, Stoics promote the principle of accepting things as they come and maintaining a calm and composed demeanor regardless of the situation.

3.2. Contrasting the Wall and the Wind

Imagine a large stone in the path of wind. The stoic is like the stone - immovable and unswayed by the circumstances. In contrast, a non-stoic may be like the wind, shifting direction based on outer circumstances. When applied to communication and speaking, this stoic tenet can result in a speaker who remains calm and composed, regardless of audience reactions or other external factors.

3.3. Control and Non-Control in Communication

Stoic philosophy stresses the division between things within our control (our thoughts, emotions, and actions) and things outside of our control (external events, other people's thoughts, and reactions). Accurate understanding of this division helps achieve effective communication.

In a public speaking context, things in our control would include our preparedness, clarity of speech, use of language, and delivery style. Things we can't control may include audience reactions, technological malfunctions, or environmental factors. Knowing this difference, a stoic speaker can focus on optimizing elements within their control and accept elements not in their control.

3.4. Stoicism and Emotional Regulation

Stoicism is widely recognized for its fundamental teachings on the mastery of emotions. This valuable skill, often perceived as emotional intelligence today, plays a crucial role during public speaking. By detaching from their emotions, a stoic speaker may convey their thoughts more effectively without being disturbed by fear, anxiety, or any other negative emotion that may hinder communication.

3.5. Articulating with Assertiveness

Another significant aspect that Stoicism introduces to communication is the practice of assertiveness. Being submissive or aggressive can negatively affect a speaker's ability to convey their point. However, Stoicism encourages balance - allowing the speaker to convey their thoughts assertively without undermining the value of others' ideas.

3.6. Authenticity and Stoicism

From a stoic perspective, authenticity is about letting your principles guide your action, not external opinions or fear of judgment. In public speaking, this translates into delivering a presentation that resonates with your own values and beliefs, which in turn, can enhance the audience's trust and engagement.

3.7. Stoic Resilience and Adapting to Change

Resilience, the ability to bounce back from setbacks, is a key stoic virtue. When it comes to public speaking, things don't always go as planned. Technological glitches may happen, the audience may respond differently than expected, or sudden stage fright may occur. With stoic resilience, a speaker can adapt to these changes without losing their focus or composure.

3.8. Continuous Improvement as a Stoic Value

The stoics believe in continuous learning and improvement. This extends to the realm of public speaking as well - whereby consistent practice, self-evaluation, and learning from each experience are considered vital.

Applying stoicism's principles can transform anyone's communication and public speaking skills. By embracing and understanding stoic values like control and non-control, emotional regulation, assertiveness, authenticity, resilience, and continuous improvement, we can elevate our speaking skills, capturing the audience's attention not by force, but with an undeniable aura of calm and composure.

Chapter 4. Commanding Presence: How Serenity Nourishes Your Speaking Skills

In public speaking, commanding presence is not only about exuding gravitas or charisma, but it is also deeply rooted in the interior landscape of calm and tranquility. This serenity is less about muting your feelings and more about being aware of them, assessing their influence on your speech, and harnessing them to serve your public speaking purpose. Here, we delve deeper into the essence of how cultivating serenity can significantly nourish your public speaking skills.

4.1. The Power of Serenity in Stoicism

Stoicism, an ancient school of philosophy, highlights serenity as one of the keys to achieving a fulfilling and peaceful life. The tranquility that Stoicism promotes is not an objective state but a method for engaging productively with your emotions. By extension, this tranquility can greatly impact your public speaking skills.

In public speaking, emotions are often the gatekeepers. They regulate the bridge between your thoughts and their articulation. They can either amplify your message if managed adeptly or distort it if left uncontrolled. When serenity is instilled in your speaking, it helps avoid emotional extremes and keeps your message clear and effective.

Serenity also anchors you in the present moment. In tenets of

Stoicism, the present moment is the only reality we can control, not the past or future. This focus helps decrease unnecessary anticipatory anxiety about your speech and center your attention on the delivery.

4.2. Cultivating Inner Calm

The path towards achieving serenity in your public speaking skills starts from within, by cultivating inner calm. This calm is not a silencing of emotions, but clear understanding and management of them. Implement these practices to perennially nurture your inner calm.

.Mindfulness: This refers to the practice of existing in the present moment without judgment. Practicing mindfulness can help develop a sense of calm amidst the storm of public speaking anxiety. You can engage in mindfulness exercises daily to cultivate this skill.

.Meditation: Regular meditation can aid in calming a racing mind. Guided visualization exercises can be especially helpful. Imagine yourself speaking confidently and calmly in front of an engaged audience. This creates a roadmap in your mind for successful public speaking.

.Deep Breathing: Deep, controlled breathing can physiologically reduce symptoms of stress. Practice deep breathing exercises before and during your public speaking events to maintain your inner calm.

By developing these practices, you lay the groundwork for harnessing serenity in your public speaking skills.

4.3. Embracing the Ethos of Stoicism

While you've begun cultivating inner calm, it's equally crucial to embrace the ethos of stoicism. The practice involves avoiding afflictive emotions (or 'passions') that could distort your judgment. Stoicism encourages discerning what's in your control, and recognizably releases what's not.

Embracing this ethos in public speaking implies understanding what you can control—your content, your voice tone, your body language—and relinquishing worry about factors beyond your control—audience reactions, technical crashes or unexpected events.

When applied to public speaking, these tenets can help create a sense of detachment from potentially disruptive external circumstances, and instead, concentrate on delivering your message with clarity and confidence.

4.4. Building a Commanding Presence

With your roots now firmly embedded in your own calm, it's time to focus on how these ideas manifest externally to build a commanding presence.

.**Authenticity:** Authentic speakers resonate with audiences. Speak with genuineness and sincerity, embody your words, and avoid artifice or pretense.

.**Confidence:** Confidence is the outward symbol of your inner calm. Show composure in your stance and voice—this communicates your authority and expertise on your topic.

.**Clarity:** Clear communication is achieved when your message isn't clouded by nerves or negative emotions.

.**Connection:** Engage and interact with your audience, make them feel a part of your speech.

By weaving together these threads, a fabric of serenity-spun command begins to emerge, enhancing your public speaking skills in a way that is both tranquility-infused and audience-engaging.

4.5. Implementing Stoicism in Your Speaking Routine

Implement the stoic practices of reflecting on your emotions, accepting what you cannot control, and maintaining a focus on your message into your speaking routine.

Before your presentation, dedicate time to mindfulness and meditation practices. Consider potential issues that might arise and accept them as out of your control. During your speech, keep drawing your focus back to the present moment and your message. After your speech, reflect on your emotions and experience.

While the techniques are valuable individually, true success comes from the integration of them all.

Serenity is a subtle force. It does not stun, it pervades. Each thread of calm you weave into your public speaking skills strengthens the tapestry of your command. The end goal is this: to step on stage, feel the undercurrent of your calm, guide it through your speech, and be your commanding yet serene self. The road to stoic serenity in public speaking is not quick and easy and calls for tenacity and diligence. But as the stoics say, - what we fear doing most is usually what we most need to do. We've illuminated the path, are you ready for the journey?

Chapter 5. The Art of Stoic Listening: Fostering Genuine Connections

As an integral part of effective public speaking, listening - really listening - has the power to foster genuine connections and profoundly shape the way your message is received. From a stoic standpoint, listening is viewed not just as a passive activity, but as an active, engaging, and impactful practice that requires no less attention and skill than speaking itself.

5.1. The Echo of Stoicism and the Importance of Listening

Stoicism, an ancient Greek philosophy, extols virtues like wisdom, courage, justice, and temperance, which are as applicable in today's chaotic society as they were two millennia ago. Listening, a key ingredient of communication, is where these virtues convene and converse. Wisdom calls for understanding; courage demands us to face different viewpoints; justice compels fair hearing; and temperance urges patience.

The stoic sage Epictetus emphasized, "We have two ears and one mouth so that we can listen twice as much as we speak." Stoic listening can be characterized as a means to acquire knowledge, build connections, and empathize with others. It emphasizes the individual's ability to control their actions and reactions, urging us to listen attentively and empathetically.

5.2. Key Principles of Stoic Listening

1. **Perceiving with Presence:** Putting wisdom into practice begins with honing our attention. This demands active presence, an acute awareness not only of words but also nonverbal cues like facial expressions, body language, and pauses. Start noticing how our need to interject, provide solutions, or jump to conclusions can often interrupt this active listening process.

2. **Embracing Discomfort and Difference:** Effective listening requires the courage to stay open to new or differing ideas, even when they challenge our deeply-held beliefs. To glean wisdom from exchanges, we must confront uncomfortable truths, even when they challenge our worldview.

3. **Activating Empathy:** Listening should encourage empathy rather than judgment. A stoic listener steps into another's shoes and tries to understand views from their perspective. Remember, we all have different backgrounds, experiences, and mindsets that shape our narratives.

4. **Practicing Patience:** Stoic listening requires patience to let the speaker finish their thoughts without interruption. Exercising patience and restraint allows us to absorb the full message being conveyed and shows respect for the speaker's ideas.

5.3. Becoming a Better Stoic Listener: Practical Tips

To elevate your public speaking skills and establish a connection with your audience, you must first become a better listener. Below are some practical tips to help you cultivate this art:

- **Cultivate mindfulness:** Practice being fully present and aware during conversations without getting distracted. Mindful listening can alleviate miscommunication and enhance understanding.

- **Avoid interruptions:** Practice silence and allow the speaker to share their thoughts fully. This tempers our impulses, enhances patience, and prevents us from jumping into conclusions.

- **Ask open-ended questions:** These encourage detailed responses and express your genuine interest to understand the speaker's point of view.

- **Provide feedback:** Summary, paraphrasing, or sharing how the speaker's words impact you showcase active listening and promote dialogue.

- **Exercise empathy:** Show respect and understanding, regardless of agreement with the speaker's viewpoint.

5.4. The Rewards of Stoic Listening

When you adopt stoic listening, you project a sense of calm and control, eliciting trust and respect from your audience. This doesn't just add value to your role as the speaker, but also paves the way for authentic connections, mutual understanding, and rich interactions.

Stoic listening is a transformative practice that complements public speaking. It allows us to understand our audience better, refine our messaging, and deliver our thoughts with increased clarity and effectiveness. Truly, the time spent in honing this art is an investment in building a poised, assured, and influential presence on stage.

In a world often plagued by noise, stoic listening offers a refreshing chance for clarity, connection, and genuine exchange. Incorporate these principles and practices into your public speaking routine, and experience the difference it makes - not just to your audience, but also to you, the speaker. Together, let's foster genuine connections and make every word count.

Chapter 6. Unleashing Your Inner Calm: Lessons From Stoic Mindfulness

Mastering public speaking begins before you even utter your first word to an audience. It begins with understanding your inner calm and how you can channel that tranquility into your presentations. In this chapter, utilizing the wisdom from stoic mindfulness, you will explore how to recognize, cultivate, and utilize your inner calm.

===The Core of Stoic Mindfulness

Stoicism, a practice that dates back to ancient Greece and Rome, emphasizes the importance of being mindful and present in every moment. It teaches that we cannot control external circumstances or what others say and do. Our power lies in controlling our reactions and our thoughts, and stoic mindfulness plays a crucial role in this.

Stoic mindfulness, as described by Marcus Aurelius, is "the ability to pay consistent attention to our ruling faculty." In more accessible terms, it is the practice of retaining control over our thoughts and reactions, whatever may come. The stoics viewed the mind as the "ruling faculty," understanding that while we may not have jurisdiction over external conditions, we have absolute control over our internal responses.

===Harnessing Your Inner Calm

Stoic mindfulness can serve as a powerful tool for harnessing your inner calm. It starts with recognizing the value of tranquility in your life and appreciating the moments where you feel most at peace. It's about taking time each day to nurture this calm, to learn how to summon it when you need it most.

A practical way of doing this is through daily meditation. Stoics often practice a form of meditation known as 'Premeditatio Malorum,' or the premeditation of evils. This mental exercise involves envisioning difficulties, setbacks, or struggles you may encounter, then thoughtfully considering how you will respond. It is not an exercise in worry; instead, it prepares your mind to stay calm and composed, no matter what.

To practice, simply find a calm space, take a few deep breaths, and visualize an upcoming public speaking event. As you visualize, imagine the things that could go wrong—perhaps a technical glitch or forgetting your lines. Now, instead of panicking, imagine yourself responding with a sense of calm and control.

===Stoic Mindfulness in Public Speaking

How does stoic mindfulness help in public speaking? It aids you in staying present and grounded in the moment. A common problem many public speakers face is either dwelling on past mistakes or worrying about the future, often leading to anxiety and nervousness.

With stoic mindfulness, however, your focus is on the current moment. You learn to accept the realities of your circumstance, recalibrate your mindset, and respond with composure. You relinquish the fear that often holds people back from speaking authentically and impactfully.

Here are a few practical ways you can implement stoic mindfulness into your public speaking:

1. Practice Premeditatio Malorum: Before your speaking event, preempt the issues that might crop up, and imagine yourself facing them peacefully and successfully.

2. Mindful Breathing: This practice helps to ground you and keep you present. Before and during your speech, pay attention to each breath that you take and each word that you speak.

3. Reflect and Learn: After a speaking event, take time to reflect on what went well and what could be better. This is not about beating yourself up for mistakes, but about learning and growing.

===Maintaining Your Inner Tranquility

Stoic mindfulness is not a one-off exercise; it's a lifelong practice. It's about consistently exercising control over your thoughts, reactions, and approach to your circumstances. Regularly practicing stoic mindfulness will help you maintain your inner tranquility, even in stressful situations.

One significant aspect of maintaining your inner tranquility is focusing on what you can control. By accepting the things you cannot change and working on those you can, you'll reduce anxiety and enhance confidence.

Another key to sustaining your inner calm is recognizing and acknowledging your progress. When we don't see immediate improvement, we often become disheartened. Remember: growth happens over time, not overnight. Celebrate your small victories, the moments where you faced fear head-on, and emerged victorious. These moments will continue to fuel your journey towards mastering stoic public speaking.

Armed with the stoic mindfulness principles, you are one step closer to becoming a confident, composed, and commanding public speaker. Embrace the journey of exploring your inner calm—that's where your unbeatable and authentic speaking persona lays dormant, waiting to be discovered. Fostering this connection to your inner self enables you to channel your inner peace into your speech, leaving an indelible impact on your audience.

Chapter 7. Channelling Your Calm: Techniques for Anxiety Free Public Speaking

Public speaking, for many, is like a colossal wave on a stormy sea. It's powerful, intimidating, and has the potential to sweep you away in a surge of fear and self-doubt. To confront this wave, it is essential to remain steadfast, harness your inner calm, and effectively channel it into your presentation. This chapter is designed to provide a comprehensive guide to public speaking devoid of fear and anxiety, centered around the stoic philosophy.

7.1. Unearthing the Roots of Fear

Before delving into the tactics for achieving unwavering calm in a public speaking scenario, it's worth examining where this anxiety stems from. Research suggests that the fear of public speaking, or glossophobia, is a primal fear. Our ancestors who lived in remote prehistoric periods relied considerably on the concept of shared goodwill within their tribes for survival. Social ostracization was synonymous with death. As a result, making an ineffective or unsatisfactory presentation in front of a large group triggers that deep-seated fear, which translates to modern-day public speaking anxiety.

Up against such entrenched survival instincts, how does one remain stoic and calm? The fact is, this primordial fear isn't necessarily a foe. It can be befriended, understood and utilized to improve your public speaking. Understanding your fear is the first step in conquering it.

7.2. Mastering the Mind: Stoicism and Cognitive Behavioral Techniques

Stoicism is a school of Hellenistic philosophy that postulates that virtue, the highest form of goodness, is based on knowledge and the wise live in harmony with divine Reason (also identified with Fate and Providence). It equips us with tools and techniques to maintain emotional equilibrium in the face of adversity. And one of those adversities is, not surprisingly, the fear of public speaking.

At the crux of Stoicism is the concept of dichotomy of control. Understanding what is within our control (our thoughts, beliefs, behaviors, and attitudes) and what is not (others' opinions, world events, the past, and the future) will allow us to focus our energy and efforts where they matter the most and where they yield results – on our own behavior and thinking.

Stoic philosophy and cognitive-behavioral therapy (CBT) are based on the understanding that our thoughts influence our feelings and behavior, not external events or people. You don't fear public speaking in itself, but rather your thoughts and perceptions about public speaking. Change your thinking, and you change your reactions.

Here's a step-by-step method to alter your thought patterns:

1. Identify Negative Thoughts: Begin by being conscious of your negative thoughts about public speaking. For example, "If I make a mistake, everyone will think I'm incompetent."

2. Challenge These Thoughts: Examine the validity of these thoughts. Is it true that everyone will think you're incompetent if you make a mistake? Of course not. Remind yourself that everyone makes mistakes bend it's not only normal but human.

3. Replace with Positive Thoughts: Replace these negative thoughts with positive ones. "Even if I make a mistake, I can regain my composure and continue my presentation. Mistakes are an opportunity to learn and do better next time."

Repeat these steps every time you face an undesirable thought related to public speaking. Over time, you will develop a mindset conducive to speaking before large audiences.

7.3. Embracing Imperfections: The Power of Vulnerability

One of the cornerstones of Stoicism is accepting the world as it is, not how we want it to be. Realize that no presentation will ever be perfect, and that's okay. Expecting perfection might rob you of your natural, authentic self. Instead, showing vulnerability can positively impact how people perceive you. After all, audiences tend to connect more with those who are human, who stumble yet recover, who make mistakes, and then learn.

The next time you're at a podium, remember, it's alright to stutter or lose track of your thoughts. What matters is how you recover and that you convey your points with conviction and authenticity.

7.4. Preparing for Success: Practice Makes Perfect

Just as a stoic philosopher might practice mental exercises, a public speaker must practice their delivery. Preparation has a significant impact on performance. Here's what this practice might look like:

1. Research Thoroughly: Read, study, observe, and familiarize yourself with your topic. The more you know, the more comfortable you'll feel speaking about it.

2. Rehearse Your Speech: Practice your speech in front of a mirror, record yourself, or perform in front of others. This will not only improve your delivery but also build your confidence.

3. Visualize Success: Imagine yourself on stage delivering an exceptional speech where you connect with your audience. Visualization is a potent tool often used by athletes to improve performance. It can work the same wonders on your public speaking abilities.

4. Emulate Role Models: Look at people who are excellent public speakers. Understand what they do well, how they manage their body language, how they engage their audience, and try to incorporate some of these elements in your style.

By making preparation a constant element of your public speaking journey, you reinforce a positive feedback loop that naturally enhances your performance and reduces anxiety.

7.5. Building Anchors: Physical Relaxation Techniques

While mental preparation is integral to mastering public speaking, physical relaxation techniques can also come in handy. Muscle tension, shallow breathing, and a racing heartbeat increase feelings of fear and anxiety. Techniques such as deep breathing, progressive muscle relaxation, or even basic yoga poses can help manage these physical responses to stress and help you maintain a state of calm.

Remember, public speaking is a marathon, not a sprint. It requires patience, persistence, and lots of practice. By embracing Stoic principles, engaging in cognitive behavior techniques, and incorporating physical relaxation methods, you can channel your inner calm effectively and make public speaking an experience of fulfillment and growth, not fear. Remember that you are bigger than your fear and armed with these tools and techniques, you can command presence through inner calm.

Chapter 8. Maintaining Composure During High-Pressure Situations

Before any public speaker sets foot on stage, there is an understanding that high-pressure situations are synonymous with the territory. Consequently, the ability to maintain composure during these moments is integral. Harnessing the stoic philosophy's guidance, we will delve into strategies and techniques to maintain a calm demeanour, regardless of the circumstances.

8.1. Understanding High-Pressure Situations

High-pressure situations are moments that trigger heightened emotions, often due to perceived risk or threat. In public speaking, such scenarios include giving a controversial talk, presenting to high-ranking officials, or speaking on a complex topic under tight time constraints.

Chapter 9. Deciphering the Inner Turmoil

It is essential to understand that emotions in high-pressure situations, be it fear, nervousness, or panic, derive from your own thoughts rather than the situation. In the stoic philosophy, it is expressed in Epictetus's Enchiridion: "Men are disturbed not by things, but by the views which they take of them". This indicates that you have the power over your emotional responses.

9.1. Embracing the Power of Perception

The key to maintaining composure in high-pressure situations lies in altering your perception towards them. The Stoics practised 'reframing', a technique to shift perspective from viewing situations as 'problems' to 'challenges' or 'opportunities'. This mental shift can significantly reduce perceived pressure, enabling composure and clear thinking.

9.2. Control What is Within Your Reach

Stoic philosophy propagates a dichotomy of control, advising focus on aspects within your control (your reactions, words, conduct) and detaching from what isn't (audience's reactions, unforeseen technical issues). Epictetus asserted, "The only thing that is truly yours is the freedom to make choices".

9.3. The Virtue of Preparedness

As Seneca the Younger quipped, "Luck is what happens when preparation meets opportunity". Being well-prepared not only boosts your confidence but allows you to retain composure during high-pressure situations. It encompasses understanding the topic, knowing your audience, practicing delivery, and preparing for potential pitfalls.

9.4. Leveraging Negative Visualization

Another powerful technique is negative visualization, where you imagine worst-case scenarios and identify ways to cope. For instance, envisage technical malfunction during your presentation. How would you carry on the speech? By foreseeing potential hurdles, you can tackle them gracefully, thus maintaining composure.

9.5. Mindfulness and the Power of Now

Mindfulness anchors you to the present moment, helping you retain composure amidst pressure. As Marcus Aurelius states, "Confine yourself to the present". During presentation, draw your attention back to your speech whenever you find your mind wandering. Breathe intentionally to maintain calm.

9.6. Handling Unexpected Situations Gracefully

Despite best efforts to prepare, unexpected situations can arise. Here, the Stoic teaching of Amor Fati, or 'love of fate,' helps to accept and adapt to the situation. Marcus Aurelius espoused, "Accept whatever comes to you woven in the pattern of your destiny".

9.7. Rehearsing Under Pressure

To familiarize yourself with discomfort, rehearse under mimicked pressure situations. This could be practicing in front of a mock audience or setting time constraints. Rehearsing under pressure not only helps you get used to the added tension, but also builds resilience over time.

9.8. Building Emotional Resilience

Stoicism encourages developing emotional resilience to handle high-pressure situations with equanimity. This can be facilitated through exercises like journaling your feelings, mentally detaching yourself from the event, acknowledging your emotions, and allowing them to pass without judgement.

9.9. Conclusion: Mastering Composure

Integrating these stoic practices into your public speaking journey can greatly enhance your capacity to maintain composure during high-pressure situations. It all hinges upon understanding yourself, redefining your perception, and making the choice, every time, to remain centred and serene regardless of external circumstances.

So, step on the stage, gaze into the eyes of your audience, and speak. In the tranquillity of your composure, every word you utter will whisper strength, and in the calmness of your demeanour, your message will roar louder than ever before.

Chapter 10. From Fear to Fearlessness: A Stoic Speaker's Journey

The fear associated with public speaking doesn't suddenly appear on the day of the speech—it's a build-up of a long-term anxiety, an amalgamation of insecurities and doubts that manifest as nervousness when you step onto the stage. It lurks in microscopic moments; that fleeting second when someone asks your opinion in a meeting; the hesitation before raising your hand in a classroom; the racing heartbeat as you prepare to deliver a toast at your best friend's wedding. We must first address this deeply entrenched fear before we can progress towards becoming a stoic speaker.

10.1. Confronting Your Fear

Stoic principles advocate the necessity of recognizing our fears in order to confront them effectively. Fear, in the context of public speaking, is usually linked to the possibility of judgment, ridicule, or rejection. To alleviate these concerns, it's essential to understand that fear is not a consequence of the situation, but of our perception of it. Epictetus, the ancient Stoic philosopher once said, "We suffer not from the events in our lives, but from our judgment about them." If your fear is rooted in the thought of being judged or rejected, remind yourself that these are external factors beyond your control. What matters is how you perceive them.

If we can train ourselves to evaluate the situation objectively, stripping it of our emotional fears and biases, we can rise above the shadows of judgment and begin the transformation into a fearless stoic speaker. Sit with your fear, understand its nuances, then tussle with it head on.

10.2. Embracing the Stoic's Indifference

Stoicism teaches us to distinguish between things we can control and things we cannot. Epictetus established this further in his doctrine: "What, then, is to be done? To make the best of what is in our power, and take the rest as it naturally happens." The audience's perception, their valuation of your speech, their biases and judgments, all are uncontrollable elements. The only thing in your control is the content of your speech, your delivery and your commitment to the message you're conveying. When you direct your energy and focus on these controllable aspects, you allow yourself space to breathe and perform without the added pressure of external validation.

10.3. Practicing Mindfulness as a Stoic Speaker

The stoics were early pioneers in mindfulness, emphasizing living in the present moment. Bringing mindfulness into your public speaking journey can ease the fear and redirect your focus on the present. It might sound simple, but for many of us, the challenge exists in truly being present. It's straightforward to get lost in an ocean of thoughts about past performances or future implications. The key rests in training your mind to focus on the 'now.'

Prior to your public address, take a few moments to practice mindfulness. Close your eyes, breathe deeply, and bring your attention to your speech. Envision yourself delivering it clearly and confidently. This practice helps channel focus on the task at hand, reducing the influence of past fears or future worries.

10.4. Adopting a Growth Mindset

Carol Dweck, an American psychologist, gave us the concept of 'Growth Mindset' - implying the belief that our skills and talents can be developed and improved over time. Stoicism echoes this, advocating that we possess the capability to learn, grow and adapt. Transforming fear into fearlessness is not a one-time feat; it's an ongoing process requiring consistent effort and dedication.

In the realm of public speaking, adopt a growth mindset by viewing every opportunity to speak as a stepping stone towards honing your skill. Take any constructive criticism or feedback graciously and use it to refine your skills. It's also important to celebrate the small victories. A smoother delivery than the last time, lesser use of filler words, a well-received joke – every little success is a testament to your growth as a stoic speaker.

10.5. Fearlessness as a Process, Not a Destination

Remember, stoicism is not a fail-proof method that ensures you'll never again feel nervous on the stage. Rather, it equips you with an altered approach to viewing your fears, enabling self-growth, and promoting resilience. The journey from fear to fearlessness isn't a linear path but a winding road full of setbacks and triumphs. The aim isn't to reach a destination where fear doesn't exist, but to make progress in our capacity to face and overcome it.

In the stoic philosophy, tranquility and inner peace are not end goals but continual pursuits. You must make constant strides towards fearlessness, knowing that it isn't an absolute state, but a recurring victory over the emotions that deter you.

The metamorphosis from fear to fearlessness is possible by confronting your fear, holding an indifferent attitude towards uncontrollable elements, practicing mindfulness, harnessing a growth mindset and understanding your journey as an ongoing process rather than a destination. The journey may be complex and daunting but remember the wisdom of the stoic philosopher Seneca: "It is not because things are difficult that we do not dare; it is because we do not dare that they are difficult."

Remember, effective public speaking is not just about what you say; it is about who you are when you say it. Be the stoic speaker; rooted in strength, calm, and unwavering resilience, you too can command the stage. Embrace the opportunity to make your voice heard, and make the journey from fear to fearlessness a transformative one.

Chapter 11. Exercises for Building Stoic Resilience in Public Speaking

Expanding the sphere of resilience requires regular and dedicated practice of specific exercises meticulously designed to embody stoicism into your public speaking skills. These exercises aim to nurture fortitude, emotional strength, and tranquility — the essence of a stoic speaker.

11.1. Daily Reflection

Starting your day with a quiet moment of reflection can set the stage for a stoic mindset. Select a quote from one of the great stoic philosophers like Marcus Aurelius, Seneca, or Epictetus, and reflect on its relevance to your life. Stay focused on this thought while maintaining a serene mind throughout the day.

Consider the stoic principle in Marcus Aurelius' Meditations 4.3, "You have power over your mind - not outside events. Realize this, and you will find strength." This sentiment is particularly pertinent to public speaking where circumstances can fluctuate rapidly. Allow this thought to guide your demeanor in turbulent times and maintain your composure on stage.

=== Mindfulness and Inward Observation

Mindfulness brings an augmented awareness of the present moment, both within you and around you. It's a practice of non-judgmentally observing your thoughts, feelings, and sensations. It's an invaluable tool in your treck towards stoic resilience in public speaking.

Begin by sitting quietly in a distraction-free room. Close your eyes and take deep, steady breaths. Next, gently direct your focus towards your thoughts.

In the context of public speaking, you may notice anxieties, fears, or self-doubt surfacing. Observe these thoughts impartially, without reacting or judging them. This practice accustoms you to perceive your emotional landscape in a stoic perspective. The more you can calmly observe these feelings, the less intimidating they become, offering you better control when real challenges arise.

11.2. Adopting Antifragility

Antifragility, a theory developed by Nassim Nicholas Taleb, is a state beyond resilience or robustness. While the resilient resist shocks and remain the same, the antifragile get better with chaos.

To adopt antifragility in public speaking, you must first change your perception of negative events. Perceive them as opportunities rather than setbacks. For instance, when encountering interruptions during a speech, employ it as an opportunity to demonstrate your unflappable grace. Antifragility is a process of active engagement with tribulations that amplifies your ability to withstand adversities and augment from them.

11.3. Present Moment Focus

In any form of communication, worrying about the past and future can create unnecessary anxiety. The concept of staying in the present lies at the heart of both mindfulness and stoicism.

To benefit your public speaking skills, practice present moment focus. Start by immersing yourself entirely in daily routine tasks - notice the elements around you, the sensations of your body, or simply monitor your breath. You will soon realize that the practice brings a sense of calm and rootedness. Bring this discipline onto the stage - focusing on your present words and message naturally reduces preoccupying anxieties, promoting effective, calm communication.

11.4. Embrace Voluntary Discomfort

Occasionally, stepping outside your comfort zone consciously can help you better cope with unforeseen discomforts on stage. Consider pursuing activities that are demanding, such as rigorous physical exercises, fasting, or cold showers.

While these acts seem unrelated to public speaking, they train your mind to remain poised in uncomfortable situations. By pushing your boundaries in controlled circumstances, you become better equipped to handle surprises in real-life public speaking.

11.5. The Dichotomy of Control

Epictetus reminded us, "Some things are in our control and others not." Understanding and respecting this dichotomy is an empowering stoic exercise.

In public speaking, various aspects are beyond your control - technical issues, audience behavior, or unexpected disturbances. Master the art of separating elements you can control, such as your content, your delivery style, and your attitude from things you can't control like audience reactions or technical issues. This practice enhances your resilience to respond rather than react to challenging situations.

These are just an introductory set of exercises to inculcate stoic resilience in your public speaking skills. Practice them regularly, and gradually, you will perceive a noticeable improvement in your ability to stay composed under pressure. You will also gain a more profound understanding of your emotions which, in turn, helps you connect better with your audience. Remember, as a stoic, the goal is not to eliminate emotions, but to strike a balance in their expression.

Chapter 12. Case Studies: Successful Stoic Speakers and Their Stories

Studying individuals who epitomized the Stoic philosophy can be incredibly beneficial to applying these principles to public speaking. History and contemporary settings alike are replete with individuals who have used Stoic principles to their advantage in delivering adept, moving, and powerful speeches. Here, we discuss three such individuals: the historical figure Marcus Aurelius, military legend James Stockdale, and sportsman-coach Phil Jackson.

12.1. The Stoic Emperor: Marcus Aurelius

Certainly, no study of Stoicism can be truly complete without examining the life and teachings of Marcus Aurelius, Roman emperor from 161 to 180 AD, who is regarded as a paragon of Stoic philosophy. Referred to as the last of the Five Good Emperors, Aurelius' 'Meditations,' a collection of personal writings, offer invaluable insights into the application of Stoicism in day-to-day life.

Marcus Aurelius was known to apply Stoicism, not just in his personal life, but also in his oratory skills. The resilience, calm, and clarity inherent in his speeches, amidst the tumultuous occurrences in the Roman Empire such as wars and plagues, won him unparalleled respect. He spoke with measured words, exuding poise and confident command over his content, thus eliciting trust and maintaining peace in the empire. Whether it was inspiring the Roman troops before a battle or addressing the Senate, Aurelius used the principles of Stoicism to keep a steady mind, avoid emotional volatility, remain fully present, and ultimately deliver his speeches with a tranquil authority that left his listeners moved and motivated.

12.2. The Prisoner of War: James Stockdale

Fast forward almost 2,000 years, and we find another incredible example of Stoicism, applied to an entirely different context. Vice Admiral James Stockdale, a U.S. Navy officer, and a prisoner in the infamous 'Hanoi Hilton' during the Vietnam War, taught us unique lessons in maintaining calm and command, even in the most horrific conditions.

Stockdale adopted the principles of Stoicism while he was a graduate student learning philosophy. He attributed his survival in the Vietnamese prison to his firm faith in Stoicism, which he called his 'survival mechanism.' Despite undergoing severe physical torture and psychological stress while imprisoned for over seven years, Stockdale exhibited remarkable resilience.

His application of Stoic principles wasn't limited to his personal resilience alone. He was able to radiate hope, determination, and an unyielding spirit to his fellow prisoners, which made him an admired leader. By adopting a mode of communication that reflected his inner calm and unyielding conviction, he not only survived the ordeal himself but was instrumental in helping many of his captive comrades do the same.

12.3. The Coach's Playbook: Phil Jackson

A more contemporary perspective to Stoic speaking brings us to Phil Jackson, the legendary basketball coach who led the Chicago Bulls and the Los Angeles Lakers to a total of 11 NBA championships. Jackson, also known as 'Zen Master,' integrated the principles of mindfulness, a concept linked to Stoicism, into his coaching philosophy; taking his teams to unprecedented success.

Jackson encouraged his players to remain grounded in the present moment. He fostered a culture of self-awareness, emotional control, and mindful action, which echoed the essence of Stoic philosophy. This attitude extended to his public speaking style. Throughout his career, Jackson's press conferences and motivational speeches for his team resonated with calm, composure, and an authentic connection with his audience.

Whether discussing game tactics, handling questions, or giving post-match analyses, Jackson manifested the Stoic ideal of 'inner tranquility.' His ability to hold attention, communicate clearly, and maintain a sense of calm even in the face of criticism or high-pressure situations exemplified the incredible power of Stoic public speaking.

By understanding and emulating the examples of Marcus Aurelius, James Stockdale, and Phil Jackson, you can start developing your distinctive stoic speaking style. You start not by practicing what they said, but by practicing how they thought, how they lived, and most importantly - how they mastered their inner calm. Next time you stand before an audience, remember; it's not about the applause, it's about the peace within you, and how you project that peace to produce a commanding presence on the stage.

www.ingramcontent.com/pod-product-compliance
Lightning Source LLC
Chambersburg PA
CBHW071049260726
48661CB00007B/3220